Selections from
The Life & Death
of Peter Stubbe

Jesse Glass

NEWTON-LE-WILLOWS

Published in the United Kingdom in 2015.
by The Knives Forks And Spoons Press,
122 Birley Street,
Newton-le-Willows,
Merseyside,
WA12 9UN.

ISBN 978-1-909443-51-8

Copyright © Jesse Glass, 2015.

The right of Jesse Glass to be identified as the author of this work has been asserted by him in accordance with the Copyrights, Designs and Patents Act of 1988. All rights reserved. No part of this publication may be reproduced, stored in a retrieval system, transmitted in any form or by any means, electronic, photocopying, recording or otherwise, without prior permission of the publisher.

Table of Contents

THE ILLUMINATED MANUSCRIPT	7
THE TEXT	25

THE ILLUMINATED MANUSCRIPT

Selections from The Life & Death of Peter Stubbe

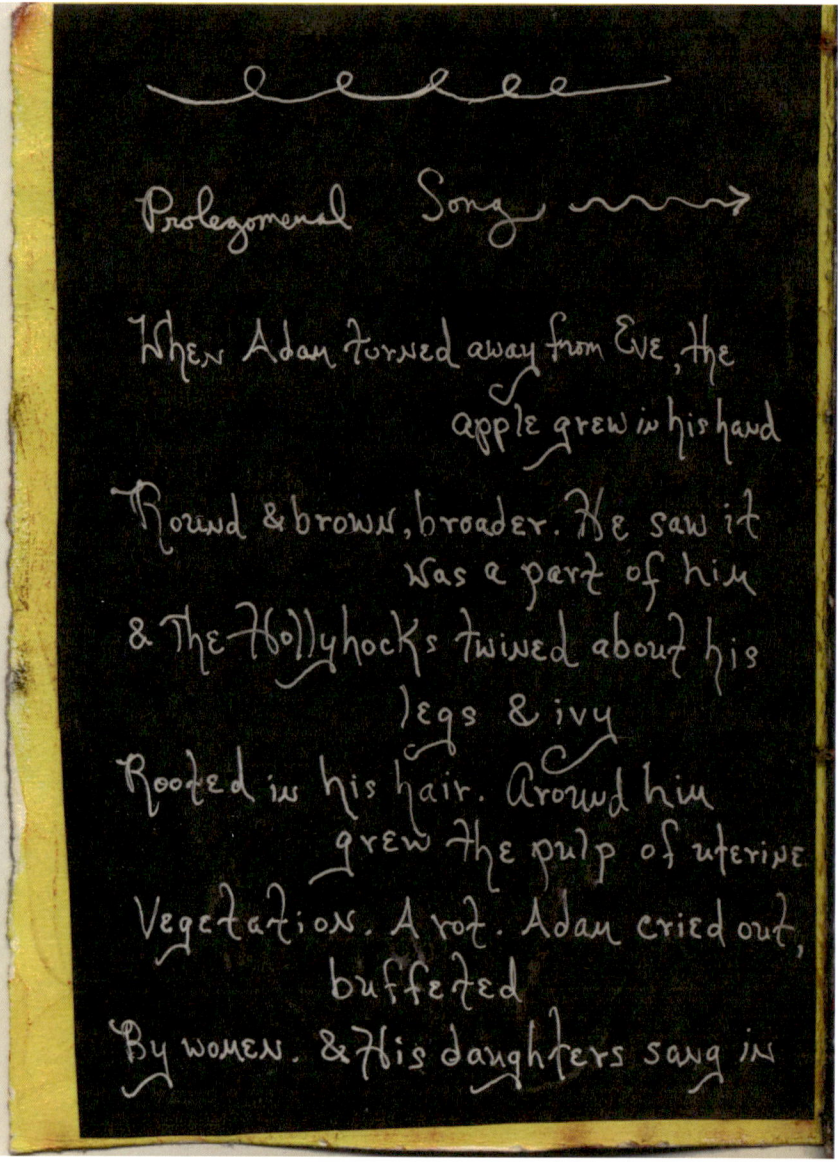

Prolegomenal Song

When Adam turned away from Eve, the
 apple grew in his hand
Round & brown, broader. He saw it
 was a part of him
& The Hollyhocks twined about his
 legs & ivy
Rooted in his hair. Around him
 grew the pulp of uterine
Vegetation. A rot. Adam cried out,
 buffeted
By women. & His daughters sang in

Selections from The Life & Death of Peter Stubbe

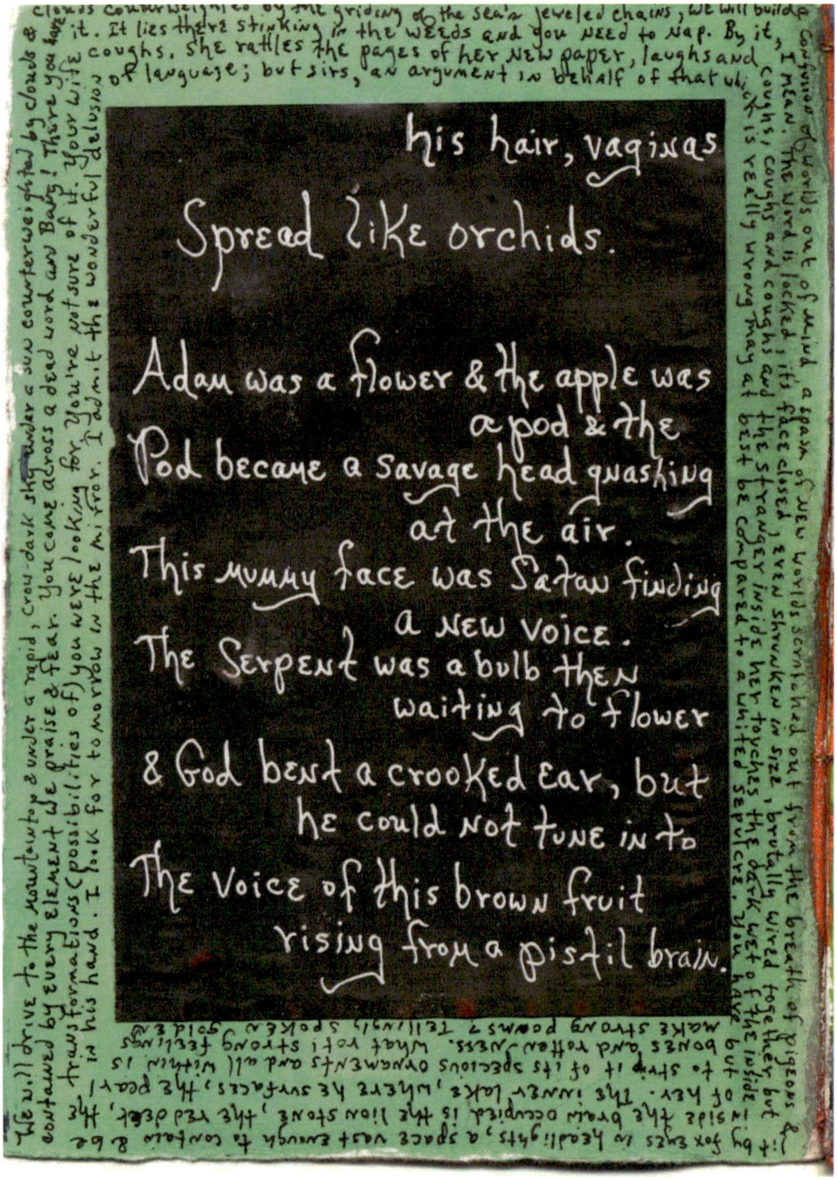

Jesse Glass

[Marginal text, top:]
clouds counterweighted by the gridiron of the sea's jeweled chains, we will build & / it. It lies there stinking in the weeds and you need to nap. By it, / coughs, she rattles the pages of her new paper, laughs and / of language; but sirs, an argument in behalf of that which

[Marginal text, right side, running vertically:]
Curious of worlds out of mind, a spark of new worlds scratched out from the breath of pigeons / I mean. The wind is locked, its face closed even shrunken in size, brutally wired together but / coughs, coughs and coughs and the strangely inside her toyshes the dark nest of the inside / is really wrong they at best be compared to a united sepulcre. We have

[Central black panel:]

> his hair, vaginas
> Spread like orchids.
>
> Adam was a flower & the apple was
>   a pod & the
> Pod became a savage head gnashing
>   at the air.
> This mummy face was Satan finding
>   a new voice.
> The Serpent was a bulb then
>   waiting to flower
> & God bent a crooked ear, but
>   he could not tune in to
> The voice of this brown fruit
>   rising from a pistil brain.

[Marginal text, bottom, inverted:]
make strong poems? Tellingly spoke a old / bones and rotten-ness. What yet! strong feelings / to strip it of its specious ornaments and all within is / of her. the inner lake, where he surfaces, the pearl / inside the brain occupied is the lion stone, the red deer, the / lit by fox eyes in keali'ghts, a space vast enough to contain & be

[Marginal text, left side, running vertically:]
We will drive to the mountaintop & under a rapid, crow-dark sky under a sun counterweighted by clouds & / contained by every element we praise & fear. You come across a dead word on my Bag! There you happen / transformations (possibilities) of you were looking for. You're not sure of it, your wife / in his hand. I look for tomorrow in the mirror. I admit the wonderful delusion

Selections from The Life & Death of Peter Stubbe

Each daughter fell from Adam's stem
& danced
Around sweet Eve, while Satan turned
his head to
Survey the fallen garden. He gave Adam
thorns
& Commanded him to die a second time,
mimicking God's

Heuristic voice.

Eve &
Adam branch &
Garden &
The dancing daughters. Death
On a snake's belly
Bloomed a third time
Then withered. A fine picture.

Selections from The Life & Death of Peter Stubbe

Selections from The Life & Death of Peter Stubbe

Listen: whispering. Silence.
　　　　Can you hear?
　　Now dreamlight. Now see this thing—
First: hoofbeats in ooze, then the hoofs
　　　　　　& a rump
Congeal in legs, hard &
Veined & criss-crossed w/ curved
　　　　　　Muscles.
Heart & bones twist from clay
　　　　& black into black
They blend,
Then the skull & the long neckbones
　　　　　　　　join
& Mud leaps over the red armature
　　　Then
The Luz falls from the stars & there
　　　　　　is brain & life:
The lungs inflate / heart trembles

Selections from The Life & Death of Peter Stubbe

Teeth click together
Eyes roll beneath their lids
Penis drops within the sheath
Each hair finds a follicle
    & The rain falls to wash him
                 free
   & He rises w/a twist of his
                muscled neck.

A black horse gallops across the
                        green
Floor of an unfinished palace.
Stubbe falls from the belly of neighing
                     Death
& Runs beside   him, first as
                    Man, then
    Flips & rolls & is Wolf
Running
              Listen!

Selections from The Life & Death of Peter Stubbe

Jesse Glass

Selections from The Life & Death of Peter Stubbe

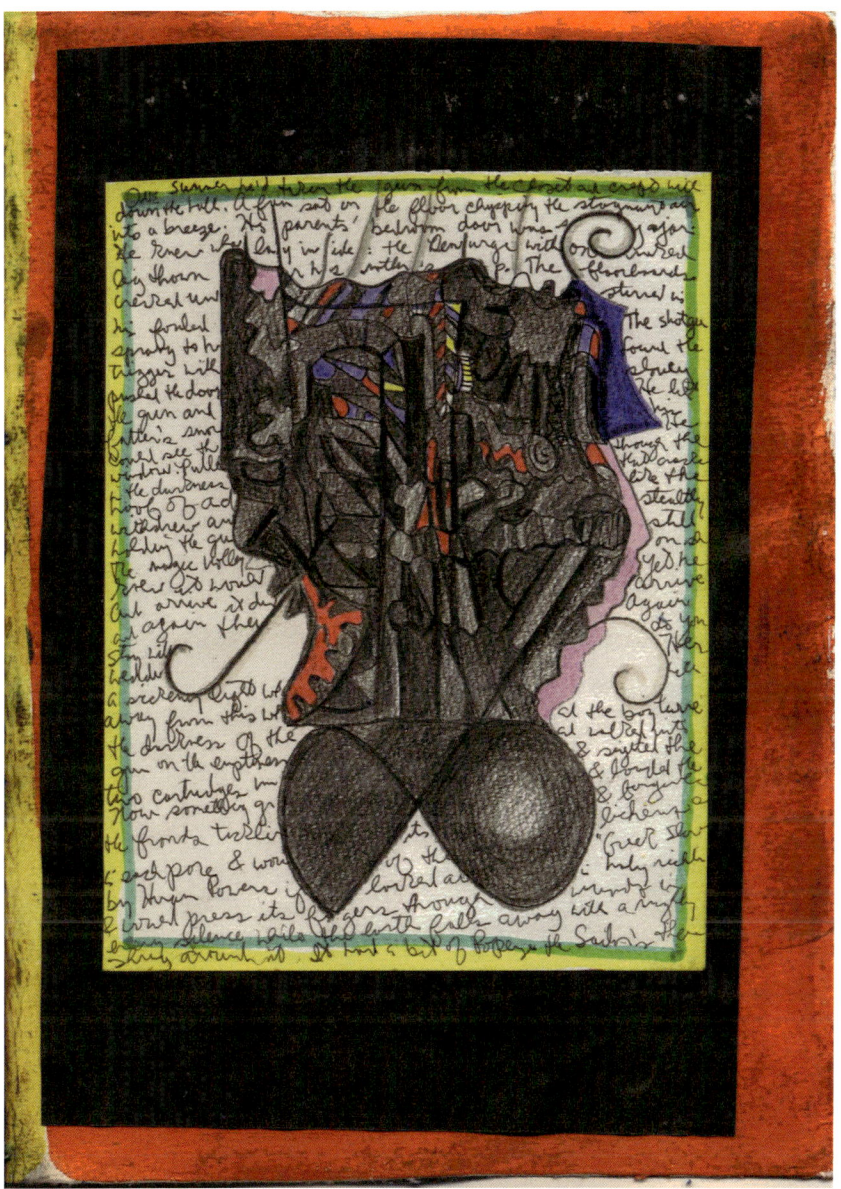

Jesse Glass

THE TEXT

Prolegomenal Song

When Adam turned away from Eve, the apple grew in his hand
Round & brown, broader.   He saw it was a part of him
& the Hollyhocks twined about his legs & ivy
Rooted in his hair.   Around him grew the pulp of uterine
Vegetation.   A rot.   Adam cried out, buffeted
By women.   & His daughters sang in his hair, vaginas
Spread like orchids.

Adam was a flower & the apple was a pod & the
Pod became a savage head gnashing at the air.
This mummy face was Satan finding a new voice.
The Serpent was a bulb then waiting to flower
& God bent a crooked ear, but he could not tune in to
The voice of this brown fruit rising from a pistil brain.

Each daughter fell from Adam's stem & danced
Around sweet Eve, while Satan turned his head to
Survey the fallen garden.   He gave Adam thorns
& Commanded him to die a second time, mimicking God's
Heuristic voice.

Eve &
Adam branch &
Garden &
The dancing daughters.   Death
On a snake's belly
Bloomed a third time
Then withered.   A fine picture.

Now is the Wolf's turn to become a lover
Wooing Eve while Adam
Suffers from a blight.   Wolf
Cock yr. leg, paint Adam yellow
For the cowards that all men are
When they see the light between yr. infinite jaws.

Selections from The Life & Death of Peter Stubbe

No woman
could satisfy
him

the devil gave him no rest.   He dragged his meat from
bed to field to bed.   His red kisses melt the flesh,
& only the hive of darkness
beyond all things

sussuration

and only the bleak edge of
light on a foggy day

quaquaquaqua

& the dead names—
a gibbering of spectral bridesmaids
& the dead names—
the bride w/ the rosemary skull/ sits in judgment upon his
prowess
& the dead

*they lie hid most part all day, & go abroad in the night,
they have unusually hollo eyes, scabbed legs & thighs,
very very dry & pale.*

saith Altomarius.

Selections from The Life & Death of Peter Stubbe

Payne

to pull
ye harmony
    fr,
ye
irregular
movements of
    Nature
(to order this poem
presupposes the
negation of jarring
actions on the nerves)

a screen drops
a screen rises

I hold my applause

        Theater
        of

Payne

in the ground
   the silver root
finds the heart

ooomaLaLLa
okLcLc
ozammazama

we take
our seats

   recognize chaos:

I CANNOT HEAR THE BIRDS

call the Wolf forth
gray about the lips
amber eyes rolling/
let him stand on 2 legs
don the mortar board, pull
the lynch pin
& explain the simple processes

   of *Payne*

to the key flower & the amaranthus
the jessamine & the musk rose
the woodbine & the hyacinth/

        those velvet, listening ears
        clapt to the sky

            push roots
            down to the recumbent, waiting
            Mistress of the Pit

            stone idol in a box of stone

            ambassadress of the sun
            to the underground

            who shrugs limbs in a
            green rolling of cornfields

            smiles in cracked mud
            the black flesh glistens
                  as she yawns

　　　　　　　　　her palms held open
　　　　　　　　　to the dripping blood
　　　　　　　　　the lounging maggot

White

curls sharp as metal
springs
stepped from the shadows
of the closet
on Sophia's sick day
--w/a finger to her lips—
& her skin smelled
       of cedar oil.
           Stubbe

ripped rags
from her belly
saw owl's eyes
blinking
& a bearded mouth grin
           red & toothless

           she

howled in
his ear, bit
his throat

    & impaled herself on his yard
            now marvelously erect.

                    no pulse in
        her neck.   cold.
                  no sweat fell
        from her brows.
                    cold.

        she rode him
        two days.

                he cried out
                under her blows

                wanting to stop/
                wanting more.

    & found that he could
    tear her apart
    like a doll
    & she would spring together
    by diabolical art
    & instantly be whole

Selections from The Life & Death of Peter Stubbe

  & bleed
  & dry & heal

      what diversion for the Wolf—
      for Man to kill
      Woman over & over!

Listen: whispering.   Silence.   Can you hear?
                Now dreamlight.   Now see this thing—
First: hoofbeats in ooze, then hoofs & a rump
Congeal in legs, hard &
Veined & criss-crossed w/curved
                Muscles.
Heart & bones twist from clay & black into black
They blend.
Then the skull & the long kneckbones join
& Mud leaps over the red armature
        Then
The Luz falls from the stars & there is brain & life:
The lungs inflate/heart trembles
        Teeth click together
        Eyes roll beneath their lids
        Penis drops within the sheath
        Each hair finds a follicle
                & The rain falls to wash him free
                & He rises w/a twist of his muscled neck.

A black horse gallops across the green
Floor of an unfinished palace.

Stubbe falls from the belly of neighing Death
& Runs beside him, first as Man, then
       Flips & rolls & is Wolf
Running

       Listen!

The men listened.   There was Stubbe's fate whistling before him:
       A long-haired comet shattering the dark—
& They saw him rising to his hind legs in that secret light.

a.

Did he confess
To all his grisly deeds?

    Of course:

        & Did they recommend his monstrous soul to heaven?

            W/ reservations.

        & before he died
        Did they pull the flesh
        In narrow strips
        From his bones

        & Break his joints
        Large & small?

            Exactly.

        & The smell of his burning,
        Was it enough to make one stop
        Attending such events?

Selections from The Life & Death of Peter Stubbe

          Hardly.

       *
       *
       *

Stubbe pulls himself from the wheel
As the poet feels the prickling
          In his scalp

Stubbe hobbles from the fire
As the poet is driven to begin

Reconstructs his flesh
For the delight of his judges
& Harangues the audience
In an unknown tongue

Full of chimes
Internal rhymes
Sliding vowels

Tells them what he
Cannot know

& Becomes pure
(As this page is
White)

& Still (as these
Words
Are black.)

Then crosses clawed hands
On his breast
& Both sinks
& Ascends.

You,
Are you finished, poet?

                    Never.

b.

& did he fly to heaven?
        the lambs the little
        children the headless
        maimed the violated

Selections from The Life & Death of Peter Stubbe

   by claw
   did
   they come to greet him
   thank him for lovely death
make him scream for hell
w/ many kindnesses?

       No.

   then did he fall
   then did he fall

   & did he escape the rude
   familiarities of Sheol
     the insinuating Duma
     angel of 100 heads
     Lilith of the tan fingers
     oozing for violation?

       No.

I remain w/ you.

Chorus of Angels

Stubbe, we bind you
        in rag chains,
you fall beneath the teeth
of presses
that crush
your body in a hail of type
        a bristling Babel-hived
intelligence within
where you/not-you
locked/unlocked
by the quality of thought
        performs
the left to right
Occidental trespass
of Meaning/torsion
of mind in matter
        that moves your shadow
then throws it back
        Poppet
manikin caged
        in a cover
        mashed grape

live on in death
your crime to suffer
a syllabled skin
the engraving pen
found in your executioner's
hand
tips like a porpoise
sonic sensing
        the form of a crime
greater than all
        literature
        now closed
        on itself
        in gigantic sleep.

www.ingramcontent.com/pod-product-compliance
Lightning Source LLC
Chambersburg PA
CBRC090821090426
42736CB00007B/241